THE LAST OF
THE MOHICANS

James Fenimore Cooper

SPARKNOTES is a registered trademark of SparkNotes LLC.

Spark Publishing
A Division of Barnes & Noble
120 Fifth Avenue
New York, NY 10011
www.sparknotes.com

ISBN-13: 978-1-5866-3475-9
ISBN-10: 1-5866-3475-5

Please submit changes or report errors to www.sparknotes.com/errors.

Printed and bound in the United States

7 9 10 8

INTRODUCTION: STOPPING TO BUY SPARKNOTES ON A SNOWY EVENING

Whose words these are you *think* you know.
Your paper's due tomorrow, though;
We're glad to see you stopping here
To get some help before you go.

Lost your course? You'll find it here.
Face tests and essays without fear.
Between the words, good grades at stake:
Get great results throughout the year.

Once school bells caused your heart to quake
As teachers circled each mistake.
Use SparkNotes and no longer weep,
Ace every single test you take.

Yes, books are lovely, dark, and deep,
But only what you grasp you keep,
With hours to go before you sleep,
With hours to go before you sleep.

Contents

NOTE: This SparkNote refers to the 1989 Bantam Classic edition of *The Last of the Mohicans*. James Fenimore Cooper did not substantively revise his 1826 text; however, in the 1831 edition, he added an introduction to the existent preface.

CONTEXT

JAMES FENIMORE COOPER was one of the first popular American novelists. Born in September 1789 in Burlington, New Jersey, Cooper grew up in Cooperstown, New York, a frontier settlement that he later dramatized in his novels. Cooper had a rambling and unpredictable early life. He attended Yale when he was only thirteen but was expelled for instigating a practical joke. His father forced him to join the Navy. Cooper began writing almost by accident. When reading a popular English novel aloud to his wife one day, Cooper suddenly tossed the book aside and said, "I could write you a better book myself!" He lived up to his claim by writing *Precaution* in 1820 and *The Spy*, his first popular success, the following year. For the rest of his life, Cooper attracted a massive readership on both sides of the Atlantic, a following rivaled in size only by that of Sir Walter Scott. When he died in 1851, Cooper was one of the most famous writers in the world.

After achieving success as a novelist, Cooper spent seven years living in Europe, during which time he wrote many of his most memorable stories. Cooper drew on his memories of his childhood on the American frontier, writing high-spirited, often sentimental adventure stories. These frontier romances feature his best-known character, the woodsman Natty Bumppo, also known as "Hawkeye" or "Leatherstocking." This heroic scout was featured in five novels, known collectively as the Leatherstocking Tales: *The Pioneers, The Prairie, The Pathfinder, The Deerslayer*, and, most famously, *The Last of the Mohicans*.

Written in 1826, *The Last of the Mohicans* takes place in 1757 during the French and Indian War, when France and England battled for control of the American and Canadian colonies. During this war, the French often allied themselves with Native American tribes in order to gain an advantage over the English, with unpredictable and often tragic results. Descriptions of certain incidents in the novel, such as the massacre of the English soldiers by Huron Indians, embellish accounts of real historical events. Additionally, certain characters in the novel, General Montcalm in particular, are based on real individuals. Creating historically inspired stories was common in nineteenth-century adventure tales. In writing *The Last of the Mohicans*, Cooper followed the example of his contemporaries Sir Walter Scott and the French writer Alexandre Dumas, whose novel *The Three Musketeers* takes even greater liberties with historical events and characters than *The Last of the Mohicans*.

Since his death, Cooper's reputation has fluctuated wildly. Victor Hugo and D. H. Lawrence admired him, but Mark Twain considered him a national embarrassment. Twain wrote harsh, humorous criticism of Cooper's stylistic excesses, inaccuracies, and sentimental scenes. Even *The Last of the Mohicans*, widely considered Cooper's best work, is an implausible story narrated in a fashion that can seem overwrought to modern readers. Cooper's work remains important for its portrait of frontier life and its exploration of the traumatic encounters between races and cultures poised on opposite sides of a shrinking frontier.

Plot Overview

I T IS THE LATE 1750s, and the French and Indian War grips the wild forest frontier of western New York. The French army is attacking Fort William Henry, a British outpost commanded by Colonel Munro. Munro's daughters Alice and Cora set out from Fort Edward to visit their father, escorted through the dangerous forest by Major Duncan Heyward and guided by an Indian named Magua. Soon they are joined by David Gamut, a singing master and religious follower of Calvinism. Traveling cautiously, the group encounters the white scout Natty Bumppo, who goes by the name Hawkeye, and his two Indian companions, Chingachgook and Uncas, Chingachgook's son, the only surviving members of the once great Mohican tribe. Hawkeye says that Magua, a Huron, has betrayed the group by leading them in the wrong direction. The Mohicans attempt to capture the traitorous Huron, but he escapes.

Hawkeye and the Mohicans lead the group to safety in a cave near a waterfall, but Huron allies of Magua attack early the next morning. Hawkeye and the Mohicans escape down the river, but Hurons capture Alice, Cora, Heyward, and Gamut. Magua celebrates the kidnapping. When Heyward tries to convert Magua to the English side, the Huron reveals that he seeks revenge on Munro for past humiliation and proposes to free Alice if Cora will marry him. Cora has romantic feelings for Uncas, however, and angrily refuses Magua. Suddenly Hawkeye and the Mohicans burst onto the scene, rescuing the captives and killing every Huron but Magua, who escapes. After a harrowing journey impeded by Indian attacks, the group reaches Fort William Henry, the English stronghold. They sneak through the French army besieging the fort, and, once inside, Cora and Alice reunite with their father.

A few days later, the English forces call for a truce. Munro learns that he will receive no reinforcements for the fort and will have to surrender. He reveals to Heyward that Cora's mother was part "Negro," which explains her dark complexion and raven hair. Munro accuses Heyward of racism because he prefers to marry blonde Alice over dark Cora, but Heyward denies the charge. During the withdrawal of the English troops from Fort William Henry, the Indian allies of the French indulge their bloodlust and prey upon the vulnerable retreating soldiers. In the chaos of slaughter, Magua manages to recapture Cora, Alice, and Gamut and to escape with them into the forest.

Three days later, Heyward, Hawkeye, Munro, and the Mohicans discover Magua's trail and begin to pursue the villain. Gamut reappears and explains that Magua has separated his captives, confining Alice to a Huron camp and sending Cora to a Delaware camp. Using deception and a variety of disguises, the group manages to rescue Alice from the Hurons, at which point Heyward confesses his romantic interest in her. At the Delaware village, Magua convinces the tribe that Hawkeye and his companions are their racist enemies. Uncas reveals his exalted heritage to the Delaware sage Tamenund and then demands the release of all his friends but Cora, who he admits belongs to Magua. Magua departs with Cora. A chase and a battle ensue. Magua and his Hurons suffer painful defeat, but a rogue Huron kills Cora. Uncas begins to attack the Huron who killed Cora, but Magua stabs Uncas in the back. Magua tries to leap across a great divide, but he falls short and must cling to a shrub to avoid tumbling off and dying. Hawkeye shoots him, and Magua at last plummets to his death.

Cora and Uncas receive proper burials the next morning amid ritual chants performed by the Delawares. Chingachgook mourns the loss of his son, while Tamenund sorrowfully declares that he has lived to see the last warrior of the noble race of the Mohicans.

CHARACTER LIST

Hawkeye   The novel's frontier hero, he is a woodsman, hunter, and scout. Hawkeye is the hero's adopted name; his real name is Natty Bumppo. A famous marksman, Hawkeye carries a rifle named Killdeer and has earned the frontier nickname La Longue Carabine, or The Long Rifle. Hawkeye moves more comfortably in the forest than in civilization. His closest bonds are with Indians, particularly Chingachgook and Uncas, but he frequently asserts that he has no Indian blood. As a cultural hybrid—a character who mixes elements of different cultures—Hawkeye provides a link between Indians and whites.

Magua   The novel's villain, he is a cunning Huron nicknamed Le Renard Subtil, or the Subtle Fox. Once a chief among his people, Magua was driven from his tribe for drunkenness. Because the English Colonel Munro enforced this humiliating punishment, Magua possesses a burning desire for retaliation against him.

Major Duncan Heyward   A young American colonist from the South who has risen to the rank of major in the English army. Courageous, well-meaning, and noble, Heyward often finds himself out of place in the forest, thwarted by his lack of knowledge about the frontier and Indian relations. Heyward's unfamiliarity with the land sometimes creates problems for Hawkeye, the dexterous woodsman and leader.

Uncas   Chingachgook's son, he is the youngest and last member of the Indian tribe known as the Mohicans. A noble, proud, self-possessed young man, Uncas falls in love with Cora Munro and suffers tragic consequences for desiring a forbidden interracial coupling. Noble Uncas thwarts the evil Magua's desire to marry Cora. Uncas also functions as Hawkeye's surrogate son, learning about leadership from Hawkeye.

Chingachgook Uncas's father, he is one of the two surviving members of the Mohican tribe. An old friend of Hawkeye, Chingachgook is also known as Le Gros Serpent—The Great Snake—because of his crafty intelligence.

David Gamut A young Calvinist attempting to carry Christianity to the frontier through the power of his song. Ridiculously out of place in the wilderness, Gamut is the subject of Hawkeye's frequent mockery. Gamut matures into Hawkeye's helpful ally, frequently supplying him with important information.

Cora Munro Colonel Munro's eldest daughter, a solemn girl with a noble bearing. Cora's dark complexion derives from her mother's "Negro" background. Cora attracts the love of the Mohican warrior Uncas and seems to return his feelings cautiously. She suffers the tragic fate of the sentimental heroine.

Alice Munro Colonel Munro's younger daughter by his Scottish second wife, and Cora's half-sister. Girlish and young, she tends to faint at stressful moments. Alice and Heyward love each other. Alice's blonde hair, fair skin, and weakness make her a conventional counterpart to the racially mixed and fiery Cora.

Colonel Munro The commander of the British forces at Fort William Henry and father of Cora and Alice. As a young man, Munro traveled to the West Indies, where he married a woman of "Negro" descent, Cora's mother. When Munro's first wife died, he returned to Scotland and married his childhood sweetheart, who later gave birth to Alice. Although Munro is a massive, powerful man, circumstances in the war eventually leave him withdrawn and ineffectual.

General Montcalm Marquis Louis Joseph de Saint-Veran,
known as Montcalm, is the commander of the French
forces fighting against England during the French and
Indian War. He enlists the aid and knowledge of Indian
tribes to help his French forces navigate the unfamiliar
forest combat setting. After capturing Fort William
Henry, though, he is powerless to prevent the Indian
massacre of the English troops.

Tamenund An ancient, wise, and revered Delaware Indian sage
who has outlived three generations of warriors.

General Webb The commander of the British forces at Fort
Edward.

ANALYSIS OF MAJOR CHARACTERS

HAWKEYE

Hawkeye, the protagonist of the novel, goes by several names: Natty Bumppo, La Longue Carabine (The Long Rifle), the scout, and Hawkeye. Hawkeye stars in several of Cooper's novels, which are known collectively as the Leatherstocking Tales. Hawkeye's chief strength is adaptability. He adapts to the difficulties of the frontier and bridges the divide between white and Indian cultures. A hybrid, Hawkeye identifies himself by his white race and his Indian social world, in which his closest friends are the Mohicans Chingachgook and Uncas.

Hawkeye's hybrid background breeds both productive alliances and disturbingly racist convictions. On one hand, Hawkeye cherishes individuality and makes judgments without regard to race. He cherishes Chingachgook for his value as an individual, not for a superficial multiculturalism fashionably ahead of its time. On the other hand, Hawkeye demonstrates an almost obsessive investment in his own "genuine" whiteness. Also, while Hawkeye supports interracial friendship between men, he objects to interracial sexual desire between men and women. Because of his contradictory opinions, the protagonist of *The Last of the Mohicans* embodies nineteenth-century America's ambivalence about race and nature. Hawkeye's most racist views predict the cultural warfare around the issue of race that continues to haunt the United States.

MAGUA

Magua, an Indian of the Huron tribe, plays the crafty villain to Hawkeye's rugged hero. Because of his exile by Colonel Munro, Magua seeks revenge. He does not want to do bodily harm to Munro but wants to bruise the colonel's psyche. Magua has a keen understanding of whites' prejudices, and he knows that threatening to marry the colonel's daughter will terrify Colonel Monroe. Magua's threat to marry a white woman plays on white men's fears of interracial marriage. When Magua kidnaps Cora, the threat of physical violence or rape hangs in the air, although no one ever speaks of it. Whereas the interracial attraction between Uncas and Cora strikes us as sweet and promising for happier race relations in the future, the violent unwanted advances of Magua to Cora show an exaggerated fulfillment of white men's fears. However, while anger originally motivates Magua, affection eventually characterizes his feelings for Cora. He refuses to harm her, even when in one instance his actions put himself in danger. Magua's psychology becomes slightly more complicated by the end of the novel, when sympathy tempers his evil.

MAJOR DUNCAN HEYWARD

Heyward plays a well-meaning but slightly foolish white man, the conventional counterpart to the ingenious, diverse Hawkeye. While Hawkeye moves effortlessly throughout the wild frontier, Heyward never feels secure. He wants to maintain the swagger and confidence he likely felt in all-white England, but the unfamiliar and unpredictable landscape does him in. Some of Heyward's difficulties stem from his inability to understand the Indians. Still, despite Heyward's failings, Cooper does not satirize Heyward or make him into a buffoon. Heyward does demonstrate constant integrity and a well-meaning nature, both of which mitigate his lack of social understanding. Cooper also treats Heyward gently because Heyward plays the most typical romantic hero in the novel, and so he must appear strong and handsome, not ridiculous and inept. Heyward and Alice, although presented as a bland couple, make up the swooning, cooing pair necessary to a sentimental novel.

CORA MUNRO

The raven-haired daughter of Colonel Munro, Cora literally embodies the novel's ambivalent opinion about mixed race. She is part "Negro," a racial heritage portrayed as both unobjectionable and a cause for vitriolic defensiveness in her father. She becomes entangled with the Indian Uncas, a romantic complication portrayed both as passionate and natural and as doomed to failure. Dark and stoic in comparison to her sister Alice's blonde girlishness, Cora is not the stereotypical nineteenth-century sentimental heroine. Though she carries the weight of the sentimental novel, she also provides the impetus for the adventure narrative, since her capture by Magua necessitates rescue missions. Cora brings together the adventure story's warfare and intrigue and the sentimental novel's romance and loss. With Cora, Cooper makes two genres intersect, creating the frontier romance.

UNCAS

Uncas changes more than any other character over the course of the novel. He pushes the limits of interracial relationships, moving beyond Hawkeye's same-sex interracial friendships and falling in love with Cora, a white woman. Whereas Cooper values interracial friendship between men, he presents interracial sexuality as difficult and perhaps always doomed. In the end, Uncas is punished for his taboo desires, perhaps because Cooper thinks he should be punished, or perhaps because Cooper wants to show that Uncas's close-minded society will punish racial mixing. Hawkeye becomes a father figure for Uncas, and Uncas eventually becomes a natural leader of men by combining the skill of Hawkeye with the spirituality of a revered Indian leader.

THEMES, MOTIFS & SYMBOLS

THEMES

Themes are the fundamental and often universal ideas explored in a literary work.

INTERRACIAL LOVE AND FRIENDSHIP

The Last of the Mohicans is a novel about race and the difficulty of overcoming racial divides. Cooper suggests that interracial mingling is both desirable and dangerous. Cooper lauds the genuine and longtime friendship between Hawkeye, a white man, and Chingachgook, a Mohican Indian. Hawkeye and Chingachgook's shared communion with nature transcends race, enabling them to team up against Huron enemies and to save white military leaders like Heyward. On the other hand, though, Cooper shows his conviction that interracial romances are doomed and undesirable. The interracial love of Uncas and Cora ends in tragedy, and the forced interracial relationship between Cora and Magua is portrayed as unnatural. Through Cora, Cooper suggests that interracial desire can be inherited; Cora desires Indian men because her mother was part black.

LITERAL AND METAPHORICAL NATURE

Nature functions both literally and metaphorically in *The Last of the Mohicans*. In its literal form, nature is the physical frontier that surrounds the characters and complicates their battles and their chances for survival. In the opening paragraphs of Chapter I, Cooper describes the unpredictability of the colonial terrain, pointing out that the cleared, flat battlefields of Europe are no longer the setting for war. The New World has a new set of natural difficulties, and the men at war must contend not just with each other but with the unfriendly land. The forbidding landscape seems even more daunting to the English because their adversaries, the Indians loyal to France, know the land so well. The skills of the English have no place in the forests of America. David Gamut's religious Calvinism, a European religion, becomes ridiculous in the wilderness.

Metaphorically, the land serves as a blank canvas on which the characters paint themselves. Cooper defines characters by their relationships to nature. Hawkeye establishes his claim to heroism by respecting the landscape. The English Major Heyward establishes his incompetence by misunderstanding the landscape. While he means well, his unfamiliarity with the wilderness thwarts him. Magua uses the landscape to carry out his villainy, hiding women in caves, jumping wildly over abysses, and hiding behind rocks.

THE ROLE OF RELIGION IN THE WILDERNESS

The character David Gamut allows Cooper to explore the relevance of religion in the wilderness. In theory at least, the American frontier is untouched by human culture. It is a fresh start, a piece of land not ruled by the conventions of European high culture, a place without a firm government or social code. Gamut's aggressive Calvinism symbolizes the entrance of religion, a European model that enters the blank slate of the New World. We know Gamut is a Calvinist because he talks about predestination, the idea that God has a plan for each person and no amount of human effort can change that plan. Hawkeye's frequent mockery of Gamut's psalmody provides the novel's comic relief. The mockery, which comes from the mouth of the hero, also suggests that institutional religion should not attempt to penetrate the wilderness and convert its inhabitants. Because Cooper makes Gamut ridiculous and Hawkeye heroic, it seems that, like Hawkeye, Cooper scoffs at Calvinism's tenets.

Gamut's fatalism contrasts with Hawkeye's pragmatism. Hawkeye adapts to his surroundings and helps the other characters to achieve improbable survivals, all of which suggests that Cooper believes humans *do* have the ability to determine their own fates. By the end of the novel the Calvinist Gamut learns to move beyond the rigidity of his religion and become a helpful and committed ally. He succeeds when he finds the ability to leave behind his fatalistic passivity and adapt to the demands of the forest. Cooper's exploration of Calvinism sets the stage for many American writers of subsequent generations. For example, Herman Melville's tragic hero Ahab subscribes to the rigid belief in fate that Calvinism endorses.

THE CHANGING IDEA OF FAMILY

Cooper uses the frontier setting to explore the changing status of the family unit. Cooper posits that the wilderness demands new definitions of family. Uncas and Hawkeye, for example, form a makeshift

THE LAST OF THE MOHICANS 🍁 15

family structure. When Uncas's real father, Chingachgook, disappears without explanation in the middle portion of the novel, Hawkeye becomes a symbolic father for Uncas. As Uncas develops his leadership qualities and emerges as a hero at the Delaware council of Tamenund, he takes on some of the charisma and skill of Hawkeye, just as a son would inherit behavior from his father. Not only do Uncas and Hawkeye form a family not related by blood, they form a family that transcends race. Despite this redefinition, however, the novel does not allow new family formations that mix race, for Uncas and Cora do not get to act on their interracial attraction. The tragedy of this sentimental novel is that Cora and Uncas cannot redefine the notion of family according to their desires.

MOTIFS

Motifs are recurring structures, contrasts, or literary devices that can help to develop and inform the text's major themes.

HYBRIDITY
The concept of hybridity is central to the novel's thematic explorations of race and family. Hybridity is the mixing of separate elements into one whole, and in the novel it usually occurs when nature and culture intersect, or when two races intersect. For example, Cora is a hybrid because her mother was black and her father white. Hawkeye is a hybrid because he is white by blood and Indian by habit. Part of Hawkeye's success comes from his ability to combine elements of the European and Indian worlds. With Hawkeye, Cooper challenges the idea that essential differences separate the two cultures. Cooper's depictions of hybridity predate the nineteenth century's extensive debate on the term's cultural and scientific meanings. The term "hybridity" became popular at the end of the nineteenth century, when rapid developments in genetics occurred.

DISGUISE
Cooper uses the motif of disguise to resolve plot difficulties and to provide comic relief. The fantastical nature of the disguises also detracts from the believability of Cooper's story. Indians who have known the land their whole life, for example, mistake a man disguised in a beaver costume as an actual beaver. These unrealistically convincing costumes are part of Cooper's move away from realism. Disguise is characteristic of the romantic genre, which favors

excesses of imagination over the confinements of reason. *The Last of the Mohicans* wants to be simultaneously a historically specific narrative, an adventure novel, and a romance. Cooper plays with the comic possibilities of romance, especially by exaggerating human appearances. Disguise therefore proves not only a practical solution to plot dilemmas but an indication that Cooper intends to make his novel partly an amusing romance.

INHERITANCE

Inheritance informs the novel's thematic portrayals of family redefinition. The idea of inheritance frequently recurs in the father-son relationship of Hawkeye and Uncas. When Chingachgook disappears in the middle of the novel, Hawkeye becomes a father figure for Uncas and oversees Uncas's coming-of-age. Hawkeye gives Uncas a valuable inheritance, teaching him and showing him how to become a man and a leader.

SYMBOLS

Symbols are objects, characters, figures, or colors used to represent abstract ideas or concepts.

HAWKEYE

Hawkeye is both a character and a symbol. Cooper uses Hawkeye to symbolize colonial hybridity, the mixing of European and Indian cultures. Hawkeye also symbolizes the myth of the hero woodsman. He demonstrates perfect marksmanship in the shooting contest held by the Delawares, for example. Hawkeye also becomes a symbolic father. Excluded from the novel's love plots, Hawkeye takes part in a different sort of human relationship by creating a father-son dynamic with Uncas.

"THE LAST OF THE MOHICANS"

The recurring description of Uncas as "the last of the Mohicans" symbolizes the death of Indian culture at the hands of the encroaching European civilization. The title anticipates the ultimate tragedy of the novel's plot. Although the title specifically refers to Uncas, it also alludes to a larger historical event: the genocidal removal of the Indians by President Andrew Jackson's policies of the 1830s. The phrase "the last of the Mohicans" laments the extermination of the ways of life native to America.

Summary & Analysis

Chapters I–II

Summary: Chapter I

The novel takes place during the third year of the French and Indian War. The narrator explains that the land itself, populated by hostile Indian tribes, is as dangerous as the war. The armies do not want to battle, and the unpredictability of the terrain unnerves them. The French general Montcalm has allied himself with several of the Indian tribes native to America and is moving a large army south in an attempt to take Fort William Henry from the British. Magua, an Indian scout, intercepts the information about the impending attack on the fort and relays it to the British General Webb, to whom he is loyal. Webb decides to send reinforcements to Fort William Henry to help Colonel Munro, who commands the fort. Shortly after the reinforcements leave for Fort William Henry, Webb dispatches the young Major Heyward to accompany Alice and Cora Munro, the colonel's daughters, who insist upon visiting their father. As they leave, an Indian runner dashes by them. Alice watches him with mixed admiration and repulsion.

Summary: Chapter II

The Indian runner, whose name is Magua, agrees to guide Heyward and the young women to Fort William Henry by means of a shortcut known only to the Indians. Soon after they leave Fort Edward, they meet a stranger. We later learn his name is David Gamut. Gamut is a psalmodist, a man who worships by singing Old Testament psalms. The mincing and dainty Gamut is out of place in the menacing forest. He left Fort Edward and lost his way. He announces his intention to join the group. Annoyed at Gamut's presumption, Heyward nevertheless shows interest in Gamut's claim to be an instructor, and asks Gamut if he is a mathematician or a scientist. Gamut replies humbly that he knows only the limited insights of psalmody, the then-popular practice of setting biblical teachings to music.

Cora is amused by the stranger. Gamut joins their party and sings a religious song native to New England. He behaves seriously and

17

venerably, as though delivering a sermon, and accompanies his psalmody with dramatic hand gestures. Magua eventually interrupts this performance, muttering a few words to Heyward, who translates his words to the others: they must be silent since hostile Indian tribes fill the forest.

Major Heyward quickly and confidently scans the forest, pleased that he sees no sign of Indians. His unfamiliarity with the forest makes him unable to see what the trees hide, and he does not notice a wild-eyed Indian peering out at them through the branches.

ANALYSIS: CHAPTERS I–II

The opening two chapters of *The Last of the Mohicans* establish war, both historical and imagined, as the novel's foundation. Cooper uses historical facts, rooting his narrative in actual, lived events in the colonial history of the United States. However, he also roots his narrative in his own imagined war. Cooper wants to emphasize the tensions between mankind and the land, between natives and colonists, and between nature and culture. He does this by using history as a frame and filling that frame with fictional events.

Cooper's characters illustrate the various ways that national cultures interact. The chronology of the first two chapters foreshadows the eventual colonial domination over the Indian frontier. In Chapter I, friendly and hostile Indian tribes rule the terrain that so daunts the whites. In Chapter II, Gamut gives a sophisticated biblical performance, ignoring the Indians as he sings. Although Cooper gestures at the eventual dominance of the whites, he also makes the white Gamut a figure of fun. Gamut behaves prissily in the menacing forest and then puts the lives of his companions at risk. Even Gamut's biblical knowledge does not dignify him; he is identified as a New England religious psalmodist only because Magua, the Indian informant, is familiar with psalmody. Heyward, although less foolish than Gamut, also acquits himself badly. He has a greatly inflated sense of his own skill and wrongly determines that no danger exists after taking a cursory glance around the woods.

Cooper's characters embody some of the broad stereotypes held during the colonization of America. Racial tensions underlie *The Last of the Mohicans*. At this point in the novel, Magua represents the nineteenth-century stock figure called the noble savage, an Indian for whom the white population feels both sympathy and horror. Whites may celebrate Magua for his willingness to help them, but they also fear his cultural differences and his familiarity with a terrain they find fearsome. Cora embodies the typical white reaction to Indians—terror and fascination. Cooper also suggests that Cora feels a sexual attraction to Magua. Attractions like Cora's, or even the imagined possibility of such attractions, terrified white males, who feared intermarriage and interracial sexual contact between Indian men and white women. This fear of interracial contact partially motivated the widespread removal of Native Americans during the nineteenth century. Cooper complicates the stereotype of the white woman attracted to the Indian man by making Cora dark, her hair black like a raven. Cora transgresses society's rules when she looks at Magua with desire, but in some ways, Cooper suggests, her desire for him seems natural.

These two chapters both begin with epigraphs from Shakespeare's plays—one from *Richard II* and the other from *The Merchant of Venice*. By invoking the lofty language of Shakespeare, Cooper announces his intention to write serious literary fiction. In the early nineteenth century, when Cooper was writing, the American novel was a fairly new form and its respectability uncertain. Cooper aims to give the American novel credence by quoting Shakespeare. *Richard II* chronicles the fall of a king, an appropriate subject for *The Last of the Mohicans*, which depicts a society that will one day shake off kingly rule and become democratic. *The Merchant of Venice* is famous for its treatment of anti-Semitism in the Jewish figure of Shylock; quoting from that play suggests that the novel will explore racism.

CHAPTERS III–IV

> *There is reason in an Indian, though nature has made*
> *him with a red skin!* (See QUOTATIONS, p. 43)

SUMMARY: CHAPTER III

The narrator shifts the focus of attention from Magua and his party to another group of people in another part of the forest, a few miles west by the river. We meet the remaining primary characters: Hawkeye, a white hunter, and Chingachgook, his Mohican ally. Though both men are hunters, they dress differently. Hawkeye wears a hunting shirt, a skin cap, and buckskin leggings; he carries a knife, a pouch, and a horn. Chingachgook is almost naked and covered in war-paint. Both men carry weapons. Hawkeye carries a long rifle, and Chingachgook carries a short rifle and a tomahawk. They discuss the historical developments that have caused them to both inhabit the same forest. Hawkeye proclaims his inheritance of a genuine and enduring whiteness, and Chingachgook laments the demise of his tribe of Mohicans. Of the Mohican tribe, only Chingachgook and his son remain. At this mention of the diminishing tribe, Chingachgook's son Uncas appears and reports that he has been trailing the Maquas, the Iroquois enemies of the Mohicans. When the antlers of a deer appear in the distance, Hawkeye wants to shoot the animal, but then realizes that the noise of the rifle will draw the attention of the enemy. In the place of the long rifle, Uncas uses an arrow to kill the deer. Shortly thereafter, Chingachgook detects the sound of horses approaching.

SUMMARY: CHAPTER IV

> [T]he worst enemy I have on earth, and he is an
> Iroquois, daren't deny that I am genuine white.
> (See QUOTATIONS, p. 44)

Heyward and his party encounter Hawkeye. When Hawkeye questions the group, Heyward and Gamut explain that their guide, Magua, has led them away from their desired destination. Hawkeye finds this explanation suspicious, because he does not believe that an Indian could be lost in the forest that is his home. He thinks his suspicions are justified when he learns that Magua is a Huron. Hawkeye describes the Huron tribe as untrustworthy, unlike the Mohican or Delaware tribes. After learning that Heyward is the major of the 60th regiment of the king at Fort William Henry, Hawkeye considers punishing Magua for treachery. Though Hawkeye considers shooting Magua on the spot, so that the traitor will not accompany the party to Fort William Henry, Heyward opposes that violence. Instead of shooting Magua, Heyward approaches him while Chingachgook and Uncas surround him. So that Magua will not suspect the plot to capture him, Heyward engages Magua in conversation. As they talk, Magua discloses the name he prefers: Le Renard Subtil (The Subtle Fox). Magua feels suspicious of Heyward, but eventually he warms to him and agrees to sit and eat. Sounds in the forest make Magua agitated, and Heyward dismounts and makes a move to capture the guide. Magua cries out and darts away from Heyward just as Chingachgook and Uncas emerge from the thickets and give chase. Hawkeye, meanwhile, fires his rife toward the escaping Huron.

> *A Mingo is a Mingo, and God having made him so,*
> *neither the Mohawks nor any other tribe can alter*
> *him.*   (See QUOTATIONS, p. 45)

ANALYSIS: CHAPTERS III–IV

Whereas Cooper uses epigraphs from Shakespearean plays to frame his first two chapters, he uses an American epigraph to begin Chapter III, quoting from William Cullen Bryant's poem "An Indian at the Burial-Place of His Fathers." Cooper uses Shakespearean quotations to justify *The Last of the Mohicans* as a literary project of high culture, and he uses the Bryant poem to ground his novel in the contemporary concerns of the young American republic. Cooper's nineteenth-century readers would have interpreted Bryant's poem as a reflection on the tensions between an expanding national culture and a diminishing Native American population. Writing in the 1820s, Cooper captures the nation's divided sentiments about President Andrew Jackson's "removal policies," which sought to move Indian groups westward and resulted in widespread genocide. *The Last of the Mohicans* speaks of the growing strength of the American spirit. However, the novel does not just cheer America; its title sparks associations with Jackson's genocidal policies. Cooper also uses the French and Indian War as a metaphor for the contemporary warfare that some feel the United States wages against Native American cultures.

Chapter III introduces the interracial friendship of Hawkeye and Chingachgook and shows how their racial histories differ. Hawkeye insists on the thorough whiteness he has inherited, and Chingachgook and his son represent the end of the Mohican line. Despite their difference in race, however, Hawkeye and Chingachgook are friends. In fact, theirs is the novel's first and strongest friendship, and with it Cooper suggests that whites and Indians are not necessarily natural enemies. According to literary critic Leslie Fiedler, the interracial friendship of Hawkeye and Chingachgook establishes a pattern of interracial male bonding that recurs throughout nineteenth-century American literature. Other interracial friendships include that of Huck Finn and Jim in *The Adventures of Huckleberry Finn,* and that of Ishmael and Queequeg in *Moby-Dick.* Hawkeye and Chingachgook challenge the separation of white and Indian cultures that was politically and socially enforced at the time Cooper's novel was published.

SUMMARY & ANALYSIS

The conflict between Magua, the Huron, and his Mohican enemies in Chapter IV shows that *The Last of the Mohicans* does not
characterize all Indians as identical in personality, as did many contemporary stereotypes. The Indians' personas vary greatly, and the
history of tension between Hurons and Mohicans suggests the com-
plexity and variety of Native American cultures. At the same time,
though, Cooper's portrayal of Magua accords with popular, phobic
beliefs of his time. *The Last of the Mohicans* thus both satisfies popular beliefs and seeks to challenge them. If Cooper falls back on
broad stereotypes in depicting some Indian characters, it is perhaps
not racism that is at stake here, but style, for Cooper creates simi-
larly stereotypical white characters as well.

CHAPTERS V–VI

SUMMARY: CHAPTER V
Magua escapes from Heyward and Hawkeye, but Hawkeye finds
blood on a sumac leaf and realizes that his rifle shot has wounded
the fleeing Indian. Heyward wants to chase Magua, but Hawkeye
resists, upset that he has fired his rifle and perhaps incited the
unseen enemy. Moreover, the others are anxious to reach a safe
place as night approaches. Uncas suggests that they retreat to the
Mohicans' secret hideout in the forest. Once Heyward promises not
to reveal this location to his English troops, they proceed there. The
noise their horses make poses a danger in the forest. When Gamut's
colt makes too much noise, the Mohicans kill it and dispose of the
body in the river. Gamut shows great remorse at this violence, and
Hawkeye respects his sorrow. They hide the remaining horses and
travel upstream toward a waterfall, pushing the young women in a
canoe. When they reach the falls, Hawkeye reflects that the horses
seemed nervous, as though they could smell wolves in the night.
This suggests that Indians might be near, since wolves appear to feed
on deer killed by Indians. Gamut sings a sad song in memory of his
colt, and the two Mohicans and Hawkeye vanish, as though disap-
pearing into a rock.

SUMMARY: CHAPTER VI
Those left behind soon see that the Mohicans have entered their
secret hideout, a cavern in the falls concealed by a blanket. Hawkeye
lights a pine bough, and the light reveals the hideout to be an island

of rock amid the streaming falls. The group eats a meal of venison. Uncas serves the two Munro sisters, showing more interest in Cora than in Alice. Hawkeye continues to worry about Gamut's mourning and produces a keg to cheer him. The group again inquires about Gamut's curious profession. Gamut and the women sing a religious song that affects Hawkeye powerfully. He nostalgically recalls his childhood in populated settlements. Amid this sentiment and calm reflection, a strange cry pierces the night. Uncas slips outside to investigate, but he sees nothing that could have produced the haunting sound. Heyward, Cora, and Alice withdraw into an inner cave for protection during sleep. Suddenly, the strange sound recurs. For the first time, Cora laments the decision to join her father at his fort. Hawkeye comes back from investigating the noise, and the others can see mystification on his face.

ANALYSIS: CHAPTERS V–VI

The Last of the Mohicans was one of the first novels to portray both the romance and the adventure of frontier life. These novels, eventually called frontier romances, became very popular in the nineteenth century. *The Last of the Mohicans* can be classified as a sentimental novel because it explores the themes of doomed love and tragic death. It is also a novel of adventure, for it portrays the exploits of frontier life. The French and Indian War frames a plot in which warfare and romance struggle for narrative attention. Sometimes the two plotlines converge, as they do when Cora and Uncas's romance begins to bud in the context of war and danger.

As early as the first chapter, Cooper foreshadows Cora's sympathy with the Indians by writing of her interest in Magua and her raven-black hair. Now Cora begins to feel attracted to Uncas. The secret cavern, an island of safety amid the perils of the forest, symbolizes the secret interracial attraction the couple feels for one another. Like the cavern, their attraction provides a comforting haven for Cora and Uncas. The physical dangers of the forest symbolize the larger cultural forces that prohibit love between an Indian man and a white woman. Just as the cavern would become dangerous if the outside world were to discover it, any relationship between Cora and Uncas would shock the world at large if it were discovered.

The secret cavern also suggests the collaboration that is possible between whites and Indians. Chapter VI makes it clear that the Mohicans rule the forest. Only they can navigate it safely. Only they know of secret hiding places that will save the lives of both Indians and white men. The white Hawkeye is able to help them, despite the fact that their knowledge of the land outweighs his; Hawkeye holds the lit branch that leads the way to safety. This fire symbolizes the collaborative friendship between the Mohicans and the white man. Hawkeye's fire has no value without the knowledge of the Mohicans. Hawkeye's fire lights the way to the hideout. Although Cooper points to the possibilities of interracial friendship, he also suggests that society will not embrace all interracial relationships. The acceptable friendship of Hawkeye and Chingachgook contrasts with the objectionable relationship that seems natural to Cora and Uncas.

Hawkeye and Gamut clash humorously. Hawkeye respects Gamut's grief over his dead colt. However, Hawkeye's pragmatism prevents him from abiding Gamut's religious singing. Rules of hunting make singing impractical. Hawkeye continually teases the psalmodist and encourages him to find a more practical weapon than his pitch pipe.

CHAPTERS VII–XI

SUMMARY: CHAPTER VII
Hawkeye believes the group has heard cries of warning, and the party hurries out of the cave. As Heyward describes the loveliness of the natural landscape, another shrieking cry pierces the calm. Heyward then realizes that the cry is the sound of a horse screaming in fear, perhaps because wolves have approached it. The howl of a nearby wolf proves Heyward right. The group hears the wolves recede into the forest as if scared off, which makes Hawkeye think that Indian enemies are nearby. Obeying Hawkeye's confident instructions, the group hides in the deep moon shadows, and all but Hawkeye and the Mohicans soon fall asleep.

SUMMARY: CHAPTER VIII
Just before dawn, the Iroquois attack with rifles and wound Gamut. Chingachgook returns fire. Heyward takes Cora, Alice, and Gamut to the protection of the outer cave. Hawkeye fights valiantly throughout the day. He believes their only hope is to defend the rock until Munro sends reinforcements. Dawn approaches, and a long, quiet watch begins. Hawkeye and Heyward hide in the thickets to monitor the enemy. Hawkeye detects four Indians

swimming dangerously close to the rock. Hawkeye calls to Uncas for assistance, and another battle begins. When an Indian wounds Heyward slightly, firing down from an oak tree, Hawkeye retaliates with his rifle, which he calls Killdeer. However, the shot only wounds the Indian.

Hawkeye's first impulse is to show no mercy, but he uses his last bullet and gunpowder to kill the Indian and end his suffering. Uncas looks for more ammunition but discovers it has been stolen by the Iroquois. Outnumbered and outgunned, the group feels defeated until Cora suggests a plan. She proposes that the men escape down the river. The Indians will not kill the women, and the men can rescue them later. Chingachgook slips into the river and swims away, followed immediately by Hawkeye, who must leave behind his rifle. Though Uncas does not wish to leave Cora, she urges him to go to her father as her personal messenger, at which point he too slips into the river. Heyward refuses to go, saying that his presence may preserve the safety of the girls.

SUMMARY: CHAPTER IX
Heyward, Cora, Alice, and the wounded Gamut huddle together in the deepest part of the cave, awaiting their capture. Outside, Indian voices shout, "La Longue Carabine!" (The Long Rifle), a name Heyward recognizes. He realizes that Hawkeye is the famous hunter and scout called La Longue Carabine, celebrated throughout the English army. The Indians enter the cavern, but they do not see the group hidden behind a blanket. The Indians express outrage at the discovery of their dead allies and frustration that they do not see comparable numbers of dead enemies. The English party begins to think they will escape, when suddenly Magua discovers them. Heyward tries to shoot Magua, but he misses. As a result of this failed assassination, the whites become prisoners, dragged outside by the Hurons.

SUMMARY: CHAPTER X
Though the Hurons at first threaten to kill Heyward, they detain him for questioning. Heyward relies upon Magua for interpretation and finally convinces his captors that Hawkeye and his Mohican allies have escaped. This exasperating knowledge nearly causes the angry Hurons to murder Alice. Before violence occurs, however, the Huron chief calls a tribal council and decides to move the entire party to the south bank of the river. While Magua takes charge of the white prisoners, Heyward tells Magua that he believes Magua sought to

deceive the Huron nation for private gain. Though he does not deny Heyward's allegations, Magua does not admit to them either. Meanwhile, Cora attempts to leave behind a trail of signals, but the Indians discover her attempts and threaten her. Magua silently guides the prisoners to a steep hill, perfect for both defense and attack.

SUMMARY: CHAPTER XI

Heyward tries again to convert Magua to their side by asking him to spare the women for the sake of their father, but Magua shows signs of intensifying malice. He quickly demands a private caucus with Cora and reveals that he seeks revenge on Colonel Munro and rejoices in the kidnapping of Munro's daughters. The traitorous Indian explains that he was once a chief, but his tribe drove him out when he learned to drink firewater. He alleges that Colonel Munro once had him whipped for coming into camp drunk and now wishes to marry Cora in order to revenge himself on Munro. Magua promises he will release Alice if Cora agrees to the marriage. Cora refuses, and Magua exhorts the other Hurons to torture the prisoners. The Hurons ties their captives to stakes. When Magua cuts off some of Alice's curls with his hatchet, Heyward breaks his bonds and attacks an Indian. The Hurons are about to kill Heyward when suddenly the crack of a rifle pierces the air, and Heyward's assailant falls to the ground dead.

ANALYSIS: CHAPTERS VII–XI

Cooper is not interested in producing simple oppositions between Indians and whites, or in drawing stereotypes. Although he classifies people by race, he also classifies them by those who respect the land and those who believe they can dominate the land. Hawkeye is a hybrid white figure who has an Indian's sympathy for nature and a white man's desire to introduce his own culture. Heyward does not have great knowledge of the forest, but he does have good instincts for it. Although he does not realize that the wolf's retreating cries signify the presence of Indians, he does correctly guess that wolves have caused the screams of the horses. Heyward has a knowledge of horses, but his white man's knowledge is ultimately irrelevant to the survival of the group. Only a figure sensitive to the rhythms of the forest, like Uncas, can keep the group safe.

Cora also defies stereotypes with her cunning and resolve. She is not the stereotypical sentimental figure of a doomed white beloved that often appeared in nineteenth-century novels. Rather, among all the group members, including the men, only Cora refuses to admit defeat. Clever and strategic, she concocts a plan that involves putting herself at risk. She likely realizes that turning herself over to the Indians, according to the rhetoric of the day, means risking rape and death, but she insists on the plan despite its dangers. However, Cooper shows the limits of women's freedoms. Although Cora constructs the plan, which gives her control, the outlines of the plan force her to relinquish control. By turning herself over to the Iroquois, Cora leaves the control of her original protectors only to put herself under the control of a new set of men.

In his exchanges with both Heyward and Cora, Magua reveals that revenge for an offense, not arbitrary malice, motivates him. Whereas in the opening chapters Cooper presents a positive picture of interracial romance, here he depicts the kind of stereotypically evil interracial romance feared by nineteenth-century American men. While Uncas desires a loving bond with Cora, Magua wants to punish Cora, and through her punish Cora's father. Magua also seems to understand the racism of the whites; his behavior may be seen as stemming in part from his anger at that racism. He understands that for a man like Munro, the thought of his daughter having sex with an Indian man would be an unthinkable horror. Both Hawkeye and Magua understand both Indians and whites, but while Hawkeye turns his knowledge to mutual advantage, Magua turns his to angry revenge and a provocation of more racial hatred.

CHAPTERS XII–XVII

SUMMARY: CHAPTER XII

A fight breaks out as Hawkeye and the Mohicans attack the Hurons, whose rifles have been set aside. In the battle, Uncas saves Cora and Chingachgook becomes locked in hand-to-hand combat with Magua, who escapes only by feigning his own death. Hawkeye and the Mohicans soundly defeat the remaining Hurons and free the prisoners. Chingachgook scalps the dead victims, while Heyward and Uncas ensure the well-being of Cora and Alice. After Hawkeye releases Gamut, they argue about the efficacy of prayer-song. Hawkeye cites the pragmatic necessities of battle to urge the psalmodist to abandon the useless weapon of the pitch pipe. Resisting

Hawkeye's logic, Gamut responds by citing the religious doctrine of predetermination and singing another song. Ignoring the performance, Hawkeye reloads his rife, and the group begins to travel northward toward Fort William Henry. Hawkeye explains that with the brilliant aid of Uncas he and Chingachgook succeeded in tracking the Hurons for twenty miles.

Summary: Chapter XIII

The party travels to a ruined blockhouse where Chingachgook and Hawkeye won a battle many years before. The memorial site spurs Hawkeye to describe the Mohicans as the last of their tribe. The group, with the exception of Chingachgook, sleeps until nightfall, when sounds of nearby enemies cause alarm. The sounds they hear are made by the Hurons, who have lost their way. Two Indians approach, but their respect for the memorial site keeps them away. After the Hurons depart, the group continues toward the fort.

Summary: Chapter XIV

The group treads barefoot through a stream in order to hide its tracks. They pass a pond, and Hawkeye tells the group it is filled with corpses of slain French soldiers. As they near the besieged Fort William Henry, they encounter a French sentinel. Heyward talks to him in French, distracting him while Chingachgook sneaks up to the sentinel, kills him, and scalps him. Firing breaks out between English troops protecting the fort and French forces, and the crossfire puts the party in danger. Thick fog conceals them, however, and they attempt to find their way to the fort through the sounds of battle. The French forces pursue them, but they arrive at the fort safely. As they enter the fort, Colonel Munro weeps and embraces his daughters.

Summary: Chapter XV

Five days into the siege of Fort William Henry, Heyward discovers that the French have captured Hawkeye. Inside the fort, Heyward sees Alice, who teases him for not seeing her and her sister enough, and Cora, who seems distressed. Though the French forces eventually release Hawkeye, the French leader Montcalm keeps the letter that Hawkeye carried from General Webb. Montcalm requests a meeting with Munro, but Munro sends Heyward in his place. The French general urges Major Heyward to surrender, reminding him that France's bloodthirsty Indian allies are difficult to hold in check.

SUMMARY: CHAPTER XVI

Heyward goes to find Munro, planning to report Montcalm's message that the English should surrender. He finds Munro idling with his daughters. To Heyward's surprise, Munro seems uninterested in Montcalm's proposal. He accuses Heyward of racism for preferring Alice to Cora. Munro reveals that Cora and Alice have different mothers. Cora's mother, Munro's first wife, was from the West Indies and was part "Negro." When Munro's first wife died, he returned to Scotland and married his childhood sweetheart. Heyward heartily denies that he thinks less of Cora because of her mixed race, but silently he admits his racism. Munro and Heyward return to the French encampment to meet with Montcalm, who hands over Webb's letter advising Munro to surrender the fort to the French. Montcalm tells Munro that if the English surrender, they will get to keep their arms, baggage, and colors, and the French will ensure that the Indians do not attack them. Munro accepts the offer and leaves Heyward to finalize the details.

SUMMARY: CHAPTER XVII

After dawn, the English slowly file out of the fort, surrounded by columns of solemn French soldiers and leering Indians. One of the Indians tries to take a shawl from an Englishwoman as she passes by. When she pulls the shawl away from him, he seizes her baby and smashes it against the rocks. Then he sinks his tomahawk into the mother's skull. Magua begins yelling the frenzied Indian war whoop, and the Indians attack the English, slaughtering them and drinking their blood. Munro storms through the battle to find Montcalm, ignoring even Alice's cries for help. Magua sees Alice fainting and hurries away with her. Cora chases after him, followed by Gamut, who has been singing throughout the battle in order to confuse the Indians and keep them away from the young women. As the battle abates, the Indians begin looting the bodies of their victims.

ANALYSIS: CHAPTERS XII–XVII

Cooper suggests that the landscape poses real danger. The characters have extreme difficulty traveling safely through the frontier wilderness. Still, the group manages to meet the challenges of nature by exploiting nature itself—they take cover under fog, for example, and walk barefoot through the stream to hide their tracks. The ability of the group to thwart the challenges of nature subtly critiques

Gamut's Calvinist doctrines, which include the belief that man's destiny is predetermined and human action cannot alter it. The group undermines this theory by forging its own destiny and manufacturing improbable survivals. Calvinism is a strict form of Protestantism derived from the teachings of French theologian John Calvin, and it soared in popularity during the first half of the nineteenth century. Both the masses and the literary elite followed Calvinist teachings. Edgar Allan Poe and Herman Melville, influential writers of the American generation following Cooper's, embraced its fatalistic doctrines.

When the party encounters the French army surrounding the gates of Fort William Henry, the novel shifts its focus back to the history of the French and Indian War. The siege of Fort William Henry actually took place, and Cooper uses historical events such as this siege to give credence to his fictional plot and its messages about race relations.

Cooper implies that Cora's own mixed race explains her desire for an interracial relationship. Although Cooper opposes racism, he makes the racist suggestion that it is more natural for Cora to desire Uncas because of her own race, whereas it would not be as natural for the white Alice to desire Uncas. For the most part, however, Cooper stresses that Cora's race ennobles her. She straddles the divide between white and Indian culture and is far stronger and more interesting than her sister.

Characters respond differently to the specter of interracial love. Hawkeye, Cooper's ideal heroic figure of the frontier, fervently opposes racial mixing despite his own easy friendship with Indians. Munro realizes that society condemns his marriage to a black woman, and while he acts ashamed of his first wife by stressing the great distance of her enslaved ancestors, he also angrily defends his wife and his daughter. Munro accuses Heyward of racism, a charge that troubles the latter. Although he denies his racism, Munro's charge makes Heyward examine himself, and he realizes that his racism goes as deep "as if it had been ingrafted in his nature."

CHAPTERS XVIII–XXIII

SUMMARY: CHAPTER XVIII

On the third day after the surprise attack, Hawkeye, the Mohicans, Munro, and Heyward approach the besieged ramparts, which still smoke with fire and smell of death. Cora and Alice remain missing, and the men desperately seek for signs of life. They find no apparent signals or codes. When they begin looking for a trail, Uncas discovers part of Cora's green riding veil. Other clues lead the men to the former location of the horses, and they conclude that the girls, accompanied by Magua and Gamut, have gone into the wilderness. Heyward wants to pursue them immediately, but Hawkeye insists upon careful deliberation and planning. Munro, depressed by his daughters' disappearance, is apathetic.

SUMMARY: CHAPTER XIX
The group spends the night around a fire in the desolate ruins of the fort. They eat bear meat for dinner. Looking out at the lake, Heyward hears noises. Uncas explain that wolves are prowling nearby. Hawkeye is pondering the meaning of paradise when he hears another sound. Uncas goes to investigate, and the group hears a rifle shot. Chingachgook follows his son, and those left behind hear a splash of water and another rifle shot. Chingachgook and Uncas return calmly. When Heyward asks what happened, Uncas shows him the scalp of an Oneida. After discussing the plan for the next day, the group falls asleep.

SUMMARY: CHAPTER XX
Hawkeye convinces the others to head north across a lake. As they travel across the lake in a light canoe, they are spotted and soon tailed by Huron canoes. The group's superior paddling tactics enable them to outpace their enemies, and Hawkeye manages to wound one pursuer with Killdeer, his long-range rifle. Upon reaching the northern shore, the men move eastward in an attempt to deceive the enemy. Carrying the canoe on their shoulders, they leave an obvious trail through the woods and end up at a large rock. Then they retrace their steps, stepping in their own footprints until they reach the brook and paddle to safety on the western shore. They hide the canoe and rest for the pursuit that will continue the next day.

SUMMARY: CHAPTER XXI
Uncas finds a trail, and the men follow it, hoping it will lead them to the women. The trail peters out and the party nearly gives up hope, but Uncas manages to divert the course of a small stream, revealing a hidden footprint in the sand bed. According to Hawkeye, the footprint indicates that Magua abandoned the horses upon reaching

Huron territory. The men reluctantly enter the enemy territory and travel past a beaver pond, whose dams Heyward mistakes for Indian wigwams. An Indian appears in the forest. Ready for battle, Hawkeye nearly kills the Indian but soon recognizes the stranger as Gamut, painted as an Indian with only a scalping tuft of hair on his head.

SUMMARY: CHAPTER XXII

As Hawkeye laughs at Gamut's Indian paint and shaved head, the psalmodist tells the men that Magua recently separated Alice and Cora. Magua has sent Alice to a Huron camp and Cora to a Delaware settlement; he has released Gamut only because the Indians thought he was insane after they heard his religious singing. Gamut and Heyward decide to secretly inform the women that they will soon be rescued. Chingachgook disguises Heyward as a clown, since Heyward's knowledge of French can help him to pass as a juggler from Ticonderoga. Heyward and Gamut proceed to the camp of the Hurons, while Uncas and Hawkeye travel to find Cora in the Delaware camp. At the Huron camp, Gamut and Heyward see strange forms rising from the grass. When they approach the tents, they realize the strange forms are just children at play.

SUMMARY: CHAPTER XXIII

The village usually has no guards, but the whooping of the children draws the attention of the warriors. Heyward pretends to be a French doctor and attempts to pacify the Hurons, who believe the French forces abandoned them. A group of Hurons returns with a prisoner and several human scalps. The Huron elders force the prisoner to run a race against the tribe's warriors in order to escape. Though the prisoner runs speedily, the Hurons outnumber him, and he wins only because Heyward trips one of his pursuers. Suddenly, Heyward recognizes the breathless prisoner as Uncas. Meanwhile, in the main lodge, the father of the man who captured Uncas condemns his son for cowardice and stabs him in the heart.

ANALYSIS: CHAPTERS XVIII–XXIII

In these chapters, Cooper ponders the moral significance of the massacre. Cora and Alice do not appear in these chapters, and Cooper temporarily turns away from the sentimental concerns of love and marriage to write about the acts of physical violence that men perpetrate against one another. Cooper condemns the interracial violence that occurs at the fort, using the distress of the characters to show his own distress. He absents the religious man Gamut from the scenes, which suggests that Cooper does not oppose unprovoked violence on religious grounds but on absolute moral grounds. No matter the time, place, or creed, the slaughter of a woman and child is wrong.

Cooper condemns those who practice violence rashly and praises those who remain calm and murder only because necessity demands it. When Heyward, Munro, and Uncas desire immediate retribution, they threaten to repeat the very brutal hastiness for which they condemn the Hurons. The measured deliberation of Chingachgook and Hawkeye counterbalances the dangers of rash action. Heyward acts like an eager, bloodthirsty schoolboy when he excitedly theorizes about the noises he hears and asks to know what happened. Cooper contrasts his yipping with the calm and sobriety of Chingachgook and Uncas, who display the scalps of their murder victims without pride or excitement. They had to kill in order to save their lives and their friends' lives, but they did so carefully, without allowing bloodlust or excitement to overwhelm them.

Cooper takes great liberties with historical events to make his villains seem more villainous and his heroes more heroic. Cooper fabricates the idiocy of the Hurons in order to make them unappealing. In Chapter XXII, Heyward poses as a clown and successfully impersonates a French doctor. Because the Hurons fall for this ruse, they appear foolish. Cooper satirizes the Indians for failing to distinguish between the science and recreation of white culture. But Cooper's ridicule is not malicious; it stems from his attempt to make his narrative more riveting, to give his readers a group against whom they can root.

The disguises that fill these chapters suggest the novel's debt to traditional romances. The British Romantic age began officially with the 1798 publication of *Lyrical Ballads* by William Wordsworth and Samuel Taylor Coleridge, but the techniques of romance—including comedy, burlesque, exaggeration, and disguise—date back to the medieval period and the fabliaux of Geoffrey Chaucer's *Canterbury Tales*. Romantic writing of the nineteenth century emphasizes imagination over reason. Although Cooper grounds his novel in historical events, imagination dictates the course of the plot.

CHAPTERS XXIV–XXIX

> *The red-skins should be friends, and look with open*
> *eyes on the white men.*   (See QUOTATIONS, p. 46)

SUMMARY: CHAPTER XXIV

Heyward searches in vain for Alice. He discovers that the Hurons, who think he is a doctor, want him to cure a sick Indian woman. At this moment, Magua appears and identifies Uncas as Le Cerf Agile. He convinces the other Hurons that Uncas should be tortured and killed the next morning. The Huron chief takes Heyward toward a cavern at the base of a nearby mountain. On the way, they encounter a strangely friendly bear that follows them closely. Inside the cavern, the sick woman rests in the company of other women and Gamut. The psalmodist sings at her bedside on behalf of her recovery; when the bear imitates his song, Gamut hurries off, dumbstruck. Heyward can see that the woman will soon die with or without his aid.

SUMMARY: CHAPTER XXV

The chief sends away the other women and exhorts Heyward to cure the sick squaw. However, when the bear begins to growl, the chief takes fright and leaves. The bear removes its own head and Heyward realizes the bear is actually Hawkeye in disguise. Hawkeye explains that he led Munro and Chingachgook to safety, leaving them in an old beaver lodge. Hawkeye tells Heyward that Alice is concealed in the very cavern in which they stand. Heyward goes to Alice and tells her they will rescue her soon. He explains that he dreams of an intimate tie between himself and her. Magua suddenly appears in the cavern, laughing in a sinister tone. Hawkeye and Heyward capture him and tie him up. Alice is incapacitated with fear, so Heyward conceals her in the clothing of the dying Indian woman and takes her in his arms. Outside, he tells the chief that he will take the squaw he holds to the forest for healing herbs. Heyward says an evil spirit remains in the cave, and the Hurons should stave it off if it tries to escape. Once they reach the forest in safety, Hawkeye sends Alice and Heyward toward the Delaware camp, while he returns to help Uncas.

SUMMARY: CHAPTER XXVI

Still dressed as a bear, Hawkeye returns to the camp, where he finds Gamut. The bear frightens Gamut until he understands that it is simply Hawkeye in disguise. The two men proceed to the main lodge and find Uncas. When the Hurons are at a safe distance from the lodge, Uncas takes the bear costume, Hawkeye takes Gamut's attire, and Gamut dresses like Uncas and resumes his place at the stake. Because Gamut's singing has prevented the Indians from attacking him in the past, he assumes it will protect him now. As Hawkeye and Uncas escape and approach the woods, a long cry pierces the night, and the men realize the Hurons have discovered their deceit. They feel confident that Indian superstition will save Gamut, so Hawkeye retrieves their hidden guns, and they hurry toward the Delaware village.

SUMMARY: CHAPTER XXVII

The Huron warriors descend upon the man they think is Uncas, although the man they attack is actually Gamut in disguise. Gamut begins to sing wildly, and the Hurons draw back in confusion. The Hurons discover the sick woman, now dead, in the cavern, along with the bound Magua. They release Magua, and he explains how Hawkeye tricked them. The Hurons, now furious, debate what to do. The wily Magua persuades them to act cautiously, and they agree to follow his judgment. The Hurons again trust Magua's intuition and passion and grant him primary leadership power. Magua leads twenty warriors toward the Delaware camp. On the way, a chief whose totem is the beaver passes the beaver pond, where he stops for a moment to speak to his animals. A very large beaver pops its head out of a dam, which pleases the chief. After the chief passes by, the beaver removes its head to reveal Chingachgook.

SUMMARY: CHAPTER XXVIII

Magua appears in the Delaware camp the next morning, looking unarmed and peaceful. He discusses the current situation with Hard Heart, the great Delaware orator. However, Magua does not learn any news about Cora, who first came to the camp as his prisoner. He seeks to please the chief of the tribe by giving him gifts. He shocks the assembled Indians by revealing that he suspects the white man La Longue Carabine hides among them. Magua reminds the people that La Longue Carabine is a notorious Indian-killer.

SUMMARY: CHAPTER XXIX

More than a thousand Delawares congregate to hear the judgment of the ancient and revered sage Tamenund, who is more than one hundred years old. Shortly after Tamenund appears, warriors bring Hawkeye, Cora, Alice, and Heyward to the assembly. In an attempt to protect his companion and stall for time, Heyward claims to be La Longue Carabine, but Hawkeye insists that Heyward is lying. To Magua's delight, the Delawares stage a shooting contest to determine which man is truly La Longe Carabine. Heyward is a good shot, but Hawkeye displays almost superhuman marksmanship. Magua stirs the crowd into a frenzy of hatred, and the Indians tie up both Hawkeye and Heyward. Attempting to gain some time, Cora implores Tamenund to hear the pronouncements of Uncas. Tamenund is lethargic and skeptical, but not unwilling to welcome the Mohican.

ANALYSIS: CHAPTERS XXIV–XXIX

Cooper makes Alice's behavior in the cavern conform to the stereotype of the weak, emotional woman. Alice's fragility inspires Heyward to declare his feelings for her, which suggests that in sentimental novels at least, men find feminine weakness sexually attractive. In sentimental novels, characters frequently demonstrate their love by performing a rescue. Heyward conforms to the sentimental model when he rescues Alice. Heyward and Alice typify the romantic pairing of sentimental novels: the brave, manly hero and his weak, lovely lady. While Cooper includes a stereotypical couple, he also breaks with the all-white world of sentimentality. He invites the reader to enjoy the adventures of Heyward and Alice but to develop greater admiration for their counterparts, Uncas and Cora. Despite their kindness and good intentions, Heyward and Alice are disempowered by their unfamiliar surroundings. In contrast, Uncas and Cora are brave, complicated, and dignified characters.

Although Hawkeye drops out of the plot for chapters at a time, he always reemerges at pivotal moments to affirm his position as hero of the novel. He occasionally pops into view like a cartoon superhero, whipping off his bear head to reveal himself or demonstrating outrageous shooting skills in a contest. Hawkeye looks even more impressive in the shooting contest in contrast to the well-meaning Heyward, who cannot quite find his footing in this strange and unfamiliar forest.

Cooper emphasizes the differences between Hawkeye, the hero, and Magua, the villain. Hawkeye proves his heroism through action, but Magua uses language to effect his villainy. Despite their differences, however, Hawkeye and Magua share some traits. Just as Hawkeye bursts onto the scene after disappearances, Magua slinks back, reappearing even after he is thought dead. One of his surprise entrances occurs in Chapter XXV, when at the pivotal moment he announces his presence with a sinister chuckle.

CHAPTERS XXX–XXXIII

The pale-faces are masters of the earth, and the time of the red-men has not yet come again. My day has been too long. (See QUOTATIONS, p. 47)

SUMMARY: CHAPTER XXX

Uncas appears before Tamenund. Uncas is serene, confident in his identity as a Delaware descendant. However, when Uncas insults Magua by calling him a liar, Tamenund reacts angrily, instructing the warriors to torture Uncas by fire. One of the warriors tears off Uncas's hunting shirt, and the assembled Indians stare with amazement at a small blue tortoise tattooed on Uncas's chest. The old man Tamenund seems to think the tattoo shows that Uncas is a reincarnation of Tamenund's grandfather, a legendary Indian also named Uncas, who was famed for his valor during Tamenund's youth. Tamenund releases Uncas immediately, and Uncas in turn frees Hawkeye. Uncas uses his newfound power to convince the Delawares that Magua has maliciously deceived them. In response, Magua insists that he deserves to retain his prisoners. Tamenund asks Uncas for his opinion, and Uncas reluctantly admits that although Magua should release most of his prisoners, Cora is his rightful prisoner. Magua flees with Cora, refusing Hawkeye's offer to die in her place even when Hawkeye offers to throw Killdeer, his rifle, into the bargain. The others, now unable to stop the villainous Huron because of Tamenund's ruling, vow to pursue him as soon as an appropriate time has passed.

SUMMARY: CHAPTER XXXI

Uncas stares longingly after Cora as Magua drags her away. After retreating to his lodge to consider an appropriate plan of action, Uncas emerges to initiate a war ritual dedicated to the god Manitou, or Great Spirit. This dance and war song center around a young pine tree, stripped of its bark and painted with red stripes. Uncas and the Delawares ferociously attack the tree, which represents the enemy. Meanwhile, Hawkeye sends a young boy to find his hidden rifles. Hurons shoot at and wound the boy on his return to the camp, revealing their proximity to the Delawares. Uncas and Hawkeye plan retribution against the Hurons, assuming the command of twenty warriors apiece. As Uncas and Hawkeye hold a whispering council in the forest, Gamut reappears, still dressed in his Indian disguise. The startled Hawkeye mistakes him yet again for a Huron and nearly shoots him. Gamut tells the men that Magua has stashed Cora in a cave near the Huron camp. Hawkeye announces a plan: he will lead his men to rendezvous with Chingachgook and Colonel Munro at the beaver pond, and then they will defeat the Huron warriors and rescue Cora. The men decide how to carry out the plan using signals and specific duties in the forest.

SUMMARY: CHAPTER XXXII

As the group approaches the stream near the peaceful beaver pond, the sound of gunfire erupts, and a mortally wounded Delaware drops to the ground. The Hurons have tracked the forces led by Hawkeye and Uncas. A battle ensues, and Hawkeye and Uncas's men manage to defeat the Hurons. As the fighting winds down, Magua retreats to the Huron village. He and two Huron companions slip into the cave where Magua has hidden Cora. Hawkeye, Uncas, Gamut, and Heyward pursue them closely.

The Hurons drag Cora along a passage leading up the mountainside. Uncas and Hawkeye drop their heavy rifles in order to move more quickly. The Hurons reach a precipice, and Cora refuses to continue. Magua threatens to kill her with his knife, but he does not know whether he wants to kill her or marry her. Just as Uncas succeeds in leaping from a ledge and landing at Cora's side, one of the Hurons loses his patience and stabs Cora in the heart. Enraged, Magua leaps at his ally but reaches Uncas first and stabs him in the back. Wounded yet defiant, Uncas kills the Huron who stabbed Cora. Magua slashes Uncas three more times and kills him at last.

Gamut strikes Magua's other companion with a rock from his sling. Magua attempts to escape by leaping from the precipice across a wide fissure, but he falls short. He just manages to grab a shrub, which keeps him from plunging to his death. As Magua pulls himself back onto the mountainside, Hawkeye shoots him. Magua stares furiously at his enemies before plummeting to his death at the bottom of the ravine.

SUMMARY: CHAPTER XXXIII

The next morning, the Delawares mourn their dead. Munro holds Cora's body, and Chingachgook stares sorrowfully at his dead son. Tamenund gives a wise speech, and a ritualistic chanting honors the dead. The Delaware maidens chant that Uncas and Cora will be together in the Happy Hunting Ground, and Chingachgook offers the song of a father for his fallen son. After the group buries Cora, Munro asks Hawkeye, who speaks the Delaware language, to convey to the Indians two hopes: that God will not forget the Delawares' kindness and that they will one day be together in a place where race and skin color are irrelevant. Hawkeye, however, proclaims that these sentiments are inappropriate and simply thanks the Delawares for their bravery. The white characters depart without Hawkeye, and Uncas undergoes a proper burial according to Delaware custom. Chingachgook laments that he is now alone, but Hawkeye argues that Uncas has merely left him for a time. Tamenund says he has lived to see the last warrior of the race of the Mohicans.

ANALYSIS

Uncas emerges as a hero in Chapter XXX, counteracting Magua's false claims to leadership in earlier chapters. Hawkeye acts as a father figure for Uncas in several chapters, and here it seems that Hawkeye has passed on to his surrogate son his qualities of leadership and charisma. Cooper suggests that the natural landscape spawns familial bonds that move beyond the constraints of genetic relationship. Also, Hawkeye and Uncas's father-son bond works in a crudely practical way, since Chingachgook disappears from the plot during the preceding chapters, effectively leaving Uncas without a father figure. Hawkeye is a useful father figure for Uncas, since Hawkeye moves easily between Indian and white cultures. It is Hawkeye, the hybrid white and Indian, who orchestrates the plan for reuniting Cora, the white, and Uncas, the Indian. Cora is not just a blank stereotype who must be saved according to the conventions of sentimental heroism; for Hawkeye, she is his surrogate son's beloved. The search for Cora becomes personal and familial because of Hawkeye's bond with Uncas.

Uncas demonstrates a willingness to play on other Indians' belief in the supernatural. For example, Uncas exploits Tamenund's belief that Uncas is a reincarnation of his grandfather. Even though Uncas uses mysticism to his tactical advantage, Cooper suggests that the mystical beliefs of Tamenund have some truth. Only after Tamenund identifies Uncas as a leader does Uncas initiate the war ritual and begin to command troops of Indians. Uncas becomes a true leader, but Magua cannot lead despite his continual attempts to gain control. While Magua attempts to win over the Delawares through oratory and racist taunting, his words do not sway the Delawares for long. He has neither the physical prowess of Hawkeye nor the spiritual blessing of Tamenund. Magua tries too hard, and he loses to men who fall gracefully, almost accidentally, into their leadership roles.

The conclusion of *The Last of the Mohicans* ties together the strands of the sentimental novel and the frontier adventure. In a satisfying conclusion to the adventure narrative, the forces of good defeat the evil Magua. In a sad but artistically satisfying ending, the stars of the sentimental novel die. Cora and Uncas meet an unsurprising fate, in some ways. Readers of sentimental novels depended on dramatic, tear-jerking endings. Cora and Uncas suffer the tragic fate of doomed love, while Alice and Heyward, the conventional white lovers, will live happily ever after. Perhaps Cooper gives greater narrative dignity to Cora and Uncas by dooming them to death; perhaps he implies that they must die because their backward society cannot accept their love; or perhaps he suggests that they die because different races should not mix.

Cooper's own position on interracial romance is ambiguous, for he offers little editorial commentary on the subject. However, Cooper's hero Hawkeye opposes interracial marriage, and as hero he might serve as a mouthpiece for the author's own views. When the Delawares optimistically chant that Cora and Uncas will be together in the afterlife, Hawkeye demonstrates his obsession with racial purity by "[shaking] his head like one who knew the error of their simple creed."

The novel ends with compassionate pessimism about race relations. Munro wants to express a hope that white and Indians will one day meet in a place where skin color no longer matters, but Hawkeye says that to suggest racial equality to the Delawares is to contradict nature. It is like telling them that the sun does not shine in the daytime. His words are ambiguous. They might be the assertion of a racist man who does not believe in equality, or they might be the defeated words of a realist who knows that these Delawares will never know racial equality in their lifetime.

Tamenund meditates on the decline of the Mohican tribe, reminding us of the title's significance. In his death, Uncas brings together the sentimental novel and the frontier adventure. The sentimental novel requires tragic love, and Uncas was predetermined to die for his passion. At the same time, in the frontier adventure Uncas plays the symbolic role of vanishing native. With him, Cooper explores genocidal white power and its capability to wipe out Indian populations. The murder of Uncas, the last member of his tribe, foreshadows the destruction of Indian culture by the advances of European civilization across North America.

SUMMARY & ANALYSIS

IMPORTANT QUOTATIONS EXPLAINED

1. There is reason in an Indian, though nature has made
    him with a red skin! . . . I am no scholar, and I care
    not who knows it; but judging from what I have seen,
    at deer chases and squirrel hunts, of the sparks below,
    I should think a rifle in the hands of their grandfathers
    was not so dangerous as a hickory bow and a good
    flint-head might be, if drawn with Indian judgment,
    and sent by an Indian eye.

Hawkeye makes this pronouncement on Indians in Chapter III in
response to Chingachgook's proposal of racial equality. Hawkeye's
words typify the novel's ambivalence about race. On the one hand,
Hawkeye expresses surprise that Chingachgook can "reason," having equated "red skin" with the absence of intelligence. Hawkeye's
insinuation is that Indians are inferior to whites. Yet, on the other
hand, a different interpretation of these exact words could suggest
that Hawkeye opposes racism. Hawkeye could mean he does not
understand why most whites think Indians lack reason simply
because their skin is not white.

Hawkeye then praises in exaggerated fashion the fierceness of
the Indian's handmade weapons compared to the power of the
white man's rifle. While he expresses his amazement at the Indians'
prowess, his praise could be interpreted as condescending. After all,
Hawkeye's praise of the Indians includes a suggestion that Indians
cannot operate rifles. Perhaps Hawkeye approves of the Indians'
skill with their quaint toys but operates on the assumption that the
whites' rifles are far superior if wielded by knowledgeable white
men. Like the novel, Hawkeye expresses tolerance and racism
simultaneously.

QUOTATIONS

2.   I am not a prejudiced man, nor one who vaunts himself on his natural privileges, though the worst enemy I have on earth, and he is an Iroquois, daren't deny that I am genuine white.

Hawkeye describes himself with these words in Chapter III when Chingachgook asks how white men like Hawkeye know about Indians. Though *The Last of the Mohicans* predates scientific knowledge about genetics, Hawkeye comes up with what sounds like a genetic description of the purity of his racial makeup. The adjective "genuine" suggests sexual purity, foreshadowing the novel's later exploration of racial mixing and Hawkeye's phobic response to the possibility of interracial marriage. Hawkeye holds mixed views on race, as these words show. Although he has strong friendships with many Indian men, here he demonstrates an energetic insistence on his own "genuine" whiteness. Although he asserts that he is not prejudiced, he shows his prejudice by implying he would injure any man who accused him of having mixed parentage.

3.   A Mingo is a Mingo, and God having made him
      so, neither the Mohawks nor any other tribe can
      alter him.

Hawkeye expresses this belief in essential identity in Chapter IV
when waiting to meet the Indian Magua. When he learns that
Magua is a Huron, Hawkeye immediately pronounces Magua a bad
man. Though Hawkeye previously praised individuality, here he
assigns characteristics to an unknown man based on his race and
sect. Hawkeye makes this judgment before meeting the Indian, bas-
ing the judgment on prejudice, not experience. Cooper seems to crit-
icize Hawkeye's prejudice, but at the same time he endorses it. After
all, the narrative proves Hawkeye right both in his general and his
specific prejudices. The Hurons are the villains of the novel, and
Magua is the evilest villain of them all. It turns out that Hawkeye
should suspect Magua of skullduggery, for as early as Chapter IV he
has deceived Heyward and the Munro daughters. Cooper condemns Hawkeye's racism, but he also writes the plot that justifies
that racism.

4. The Hurons love their friends the Delawares. . . . Why
   should they not? They are colored by the same sun,
   and their just men will hunt in the same grounds after
   death. The redskins should be friends, and look with
   open eyes on the white men.

Magua speaks these words in Chapter XXVIII in an attempt to race-
bait and anger the Delaware council. In the novel, racist whites
often argue for unity in the face of their sneaky foes, the Indians.
Here, Magua uses the same argument against the whites. He argues
that the same sun shines on all Indian cultures, and Indians should
unite against the untrustworthy white man. Magua turns the stereotype on its head by suggesting that the Indians, not the whites, have
something to fear from a shiftless race. Cooper presents Magua's
words as nothing more than a calculated attempt to stir up the emo-
tions of the Delawares. However, outside the world of the novel,
Magua's words take on another meaning. Cooper wrote during a
time when the U.S. government carried out a policy of exterminat-
ing Native American peoples. Although Magua speaks from personal malice, the words he speaks should be heeded by all Indians
who must live in fear of the conquest of their white oppressors.

5.   The pale-faces are masters of the earth, and the time
      of the red-men has not yet come again. My day has
      been too long.

The Delaware patriarch Tamenund speaks these words in the final
chapter of the novel, lamenting Uncas's death. His words clarify
the meaning of the title *The Last of the Mohicans*. Tamenund
describes the pain of his old age. He has lived through three generations of Delaware warriors and has witnessed the death of the
"last of the Mohicans"; survival has become not a triumph but a
burden. You live too long, he suggests, when you are able to wit-
ness the extinction of an entire group of people. Although
Tamenund speaks mournfully, a spark of hope comes from the
words "not yet." Tamenund implies that though the white men
now dominate the land, the progress of history is cyclical and that
the Indian people will eventually rise to power again.

KEY FACTS

FULL TITLE
The Last of the Mohicans

AUTHOR
James Fenimore Cooper

TYPE OF WORK
Novel

GENRE
Sentimental novel, adventure novel, frontier romance

LANGUAGE
English

TIME AND PLACE WRITTEN
1826, Europe

DATE OF FIRST PUBLICATION
1826

PUBLISHER
Carey & Lea of Philadelphia

NARRATOR
Anonymous

POINT OF VIEW
Third person. The narrator follows the actions of several characters at once, especially during combat scenes. He describes characters objectively but periodically makes reference to his own writing.

TONE
Ornate, solemn, sentimental, occasionally poetic

TENSE
Past

SETTING (TIME)
Several days from late July to mid-August 1757, during the French and Indian War

SETTING (PLACE)
The American wilderness frontier in what will become New York State .

PROTAGONIST
Hawkeye

MAJOR CONFLICT
The English battle the French and their Indian allies; Uncas helps his English friends resist Magua and the Hurons.

RISING ACTION
Magua captures Cora and Alice, beginning a series of adventures for the English characters, who try to rescue the women.

CLIMAX
Uncas triumphs over Magua in the Delaware council of Tamenund in Chapter XXX.

FALLING ACTION
Magua dies; Cora and Uncas are torn apart.

THEMES
The consequences of interracial love and friendship; literal and metaphorical nature; the role of religion in the wilderness; the changing idea of family

MOTIFS
Hybridity; disguise; inheritance

SYMBOLS
Hawkeye; "the last of the Mohicans"

FORESHADOWING
Cora's unexpected attraction to Magua in Chapter I; Magua's deceit in Chapter I; Chingachgook's reference to Uncas as the "last of the Mohicans" in Chapter II.

KEY FACTS

STUDY QUESTIONS & ESSAY TOPICS

STUDY QUESTIONS

1.   *How does* The Last of the Mohicans *bring together elements of the sentimental novel and the frontier adventure story?*

Cooper weaves together elements of the sentimental novel, such as love and marriage, and elements of the frontier adventure, such as warfare and racial conflict. He creates friendships and psychological tensions among his characters that are typical of both genres. Cooper emphasizes the various happy, tragic, and romantic results of intercultural mingling. He uses female characters to carry the narrative weight of sentimentality, but he also introduces them into the combat situations that define the frontier adventure. Cooper makes warfare more dramatic and emotional by imbuing it with sentimental elements of romance. He heightens the novel's drama by pitting the Indian figure of good, Uncas, against the Indian figure of evil, Magua, in a contest for the love of a white girl, Cora Munro. Cooper uses the two men's interracial desires, so different in intent and tone, to give psychological depth to the otherwise simple opposition between white and Indian. Cooper thus creates a hybrid genre, frontier romance, by linking sentiment and war.

2.   *Discuss the relationship between history and fiction in*
     The Last of the Mohicans. *How do historical events relate*
     to the literary genres that classify Cooper's novel?

While the actual historical event of the French and Indian War
(1757) frames this novel, Cooper uses history primarily as a spring-
board for the imagined relationships among his fictional characters.
Moreover, the historical setting is not realistic. Cooper might mention one or two real battles, but he intentionally tempers this realism
with such devices as outlandish disguises and improbable last-
minute heroics. Cooper includes the comic effects of Hawkeye
dressed as a bear and Chingachgook disguised as a beaver. *The Last
of the Mohicans* is a romance, a genre deriving from the British
Romantic movement of the early nineteenth century that emphasizes imagination over reason and allows for comedy. Cooper uses
history as a frame and fills it with the imaginative movements of the
romance plot.

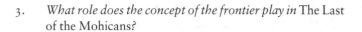

3.   *What role does the concept of the frontier play in* The Last
      of the Mohicans?

For Europeans, the frontier was almost uncharted territory, land
not yet controlled by a government or divided up into parcels. The
wilds of the frontier seem to inspire illicit desires, such as Uncas's
and Cora's desire for one another. It also seems an appropriate
backdrop for outbreaks of violence such as the Indians' sudden
massacre of the English at Fort William Henry. The frontier allows
for communion with nature. Hawkeye lives the idealized version
of frontier life. A mixture of white and Indian cultures, Hawkeye
lives according to the natural rhythms of the landscape, which
encourage and celebrate his long-lasting friendship with the Mohican Chingachgook. *The Last of the Mohicans* prizes nature over
European civilization.

SUGGESTED ESSAY TOPICS

1. The Native Americans in Cooper's novel seem either entirely good (Uncas and Chingachgook) or entirely evil (Magua and most of the Hurons). Are there any believable Indian characters in the novel? Is Cooper guilty of invoking racial stereotypes in his portrayal of Indians?

2. Compare and contrast the father-son relationship of Chingachgook and Uncas with the father-daughter relationship of Munro and his daughters.

3. In what way is Hawkeye the hero of the book? As the hero, why isn't Hawkeye involved in either of the novel's love stories?

4. Discuss three examples of the clash between races or cultures. What do the three examples show about Cooper's views on racism?

5. The nineteenth-century language of the novel can seem excessively formal and elaborate to modern readers. Do you think the novel's language interferes with the excitement of its story? Why or why not?

Review & Resources

Quiz

1. In what year does *The Last of the Mohicans* take place?

   A. 1757
   B. 1800
   C. 1826
   D. 1950

2. Who is the leader of the French forces?

   A. Montcalm
   B. Webb
   C. Heyward
   D. Hawkeye

3. Who is the commander of Fort William Henry?

   A. Heyward
   B. Webb
   C. Montcalm
   D. Munro

4. Who claims to know of a secret path from Fort Edward to Fort William Henry?

   A. Magua
   B. Heyward
   C. Chingachgook
   D. Hawkeye

5. What does "Le Renard Subtil" mean in English?

   A. The bashful student
   B. The curious renegade
   C. The long rifle
   D. The subtle fox

6.   Who disguises himself as a bear?

  A.   Hawkeye
  B.   Chingachgook
  C.   Gamut
  D.   Heyward

7.   Though he is dressed as a clown, what does Gamut pretend to be for the benefit of the Hurons?

  A.   A lawyer
  B.   A teacher
  C.   A doctor
  D.   An engineer

8.   Cora's hair is compared to the color of which bird?

  A.   Cardinal
  B.   Raven
  C.   Bluejay
  D.   Starling

9.   Who disguises himself as a beaver?

  A.   Chingachgook
  B.   Heyward
  C.   Hawkeye
  D.   Gamut

10.   Where did Munro meet Cora's mother?

  A.   England
  B.   France
  C.   Indonesia
  D.   The West Indies

11.   Roughly how old is Tamenund, the patriarch of the Delawares?

  A.   20
  B.   50
  C.   100
  D.   300

12. Which feature of the landscape does Uncas use to discover Magua's footprints?

   A. A plateau
   B. A reservoir
   C. A mountain
   D. A stream

13. What is Hawkeye's real name?

   A. James Fenimore Cooper
   B. James K. Polk
   C. Natty Bumppo
   D. Nat King Cole

14. Which weapon does *not* appear in *The Last of the Mohicans*?

   A. Slingshot
   B. Rifle
   C. Hand grenade
   D. Tomahawk

15. Of the following characters, who is the lone survivor at the end of the story?

   A. Munro
   B. Magua
   C. Cora
   D. Uncas

16. Which of the following characters is youngest?

   A. Tamenund
   B. Hawkeye
   C. Alice
   D. Cora

REVIEW & RESOURCES

17. After capturing Alice, Magua sends her to which Indian camp?

   A. Delawares
   B. Cherokees
   C. Hurons
   D. Apaches

18. Which character is nicknamed Le Cerf Agile?

   A. Uncas
   B. Magua
   C. Hawkeye
   D. Montcalm

19. How many times does Hawkeye nearly kill Gamut when he is dressed as an Indian?

   A. Once
   B. Twice
   C. Three times
   D. Never

20. In order to determine the identity of La Longue Carabine, the Delawares stage which contest?

   A. Shooting
   B. Foot race
   C. Javelin-throwing
   D. Tree-climbing

21. In addition to English, which language does Heyward speak?

   A. German
   B. Delaware
   C. Italian
   D. French

22. Which French nickname does *not* appear in *The Last of the Mohicans*?

    A. Le Renard Subtil
    B. Le Furieux Cheval
    C. La Longue Carabine
    D. Le Gros Serpent

23. Which animal does *not* appear in *The Last of the Mohicans*?

    A. Beaver
    B. Horse
    C. Turtle
    D. Porcupine

24. Which profession does *not* appear in *The Last of the Mohicans*?

    A. Lawyer
    B. Doctor
    C. Singer
    D. Hunter

25. Of the following characters, who survives the longest?

    A. Cora
    B. Uncas
    C. The sick Indian squaw
    D. Magua

ANSWER KEY:
1: A; 2: A; 3: D; 4: A; 5: D; 6: A; 7: C; 8: B; 9: A; 10: D;
11: C; 12: D; 13: C; 14: C; 15: A; 16: C; 17: C; 18: A; 19: B;
20: A; 21: D; 22: B; 23: D; 24: A; 25: D

SUGGESTIONS FOR FURTHER READING

BELLIN, JOSHUA DAVID. *The Demon of the Continent: Indians and the Shaping of American Literature.* Philadelphia: University of Pennsylvania Press, 2001.

CLARK, ROBERT, ed. *James Fenimore Cooper: New Critical Essays.* London: Vision Press, 1985.

COOPER, JAMES FENIMORE. *The Letters and Journals of James Fenimore Cooper.* Edited by James Beard. Cambridge, Massachusetts: Harvard University Press, 1960.

DARNELL, DONALD. *James Fenimore Cooper: Novelist of Manners.* Newark: University of Delaware Press, 1993.

DEKKER, GEORGE. *James Fenimore Cooper: The American Scott.* New York: Barnes and Noble, 1967.

LAWRENCE, D. H. *Studies in Classic American Literature.* New York: Doubleday and Company, 1961.

MCWILLIAMS, JOHN. THE LAST OF THE MOHICANS: *Civil Savagery and Savage Civility.* New York: Twayne Publishers, 1995.

WALKER, WARREN. *James Fenimore Cooper: An Introduction and Interpretation.* New York: Barnes and Noble, 1962.

A Note on the Type

The typeface used in SparkNotes study guides is Sabon, created by master typographer Jan Tschichold in 1964. Tschichold revolutionized the field of graphic design twice: first with his use of asymmetrical layouts and sanserif type in the 1930s when he was affiliated with the Bauhaus, then by abandoning assymetry and calling for a return to the classic ideals of design. Sabon, his only extant typeface, is emblematic of his latter program: Tschichold's design is a recreation of the types made by Claude Garamond, the great French typographer of the Renaissance, and his contemporary Robert Granjon. Fittingly, it is named for Garamond's apprentice, Jacques Sabon.

SparkNotes
Test Preparation
Guides

The SparkNotes team figured it was time to cut standardized tests down to size. We've studied the tests for you, so that SparkNotes test prep guides are:

Smarter:
Packed with critical-thinking skills and test-
taking strategies that will improve your score.

Better:
Fully up to date, covering all new features of the tests,
with study tips on every type of question.

Faster:
Our books cover exactly what you need to
know for the test. No more, no less.

SparkNotes Study Guides: